Love Lessons:
Series

I'VE DECIDED TO LIVE

Healing From Emotional Trauma, Breakups, and Betrayal

Dr. Donnie & LaToya Neal

Donnie and LaToya Neal

I've Decided to Live

Printed by Donnie Neal Ministries

Printed in the United States of America
I've Decided to Live
Healing From Emotional Trauma, Breakups, and Betrayal

First Printing Edition, 2022
ISBN: 9798836611538

Donnie and LaToya Neal

Table of Contents

PREFACE

If you are reading this book, you're probably looking for emotional healing of some sort. You may even be wondering if it is possible. The answer is yes—emotional healing is always possible, if you are open to releasing expectations about what the experience will be like or what it will lead to.

The reality is that you will never be the same person as you were before whatever happened that you are healing from. That can feel scary, but that can also feel incredibly freeing as you attempt to find yourself and experience post-traumatic growth. Emotional healing is the process of acknowledging, allowing, accepting, integrating, and processing painful life experiences and strong emotions. It may involve empathy, self-regulation, self-compassion, self-acceptance, mindfulness, and integration.

Many people tend to want to control the process of emotional healing by minimizing the pain and controlling their emotions, but this can inhibit the process of emotional healing.

Emotional healing takes the time that it takes—which may be longer or shorter than you expect or plan on—if you allow it to be fully acknowledged, felt, moved through, and processed.

Emotional healing will look different for everybody, but it may include <u>emotional regulation skills</u>, a feeling of lightness, and stronger relationships as you are able to be more present with yourself and your loved ones.

When Do You Need Emotional Healing?

All people will need emotional healing at some point during their lives—we all experience challenges and difficult emotions that need processing.

Get ready to recover, I am a witness that you can, and you will survive, recover, and be whole. It's nothing of your own, but with wisdom and the help of God, all things are possible.

What is this all about?

Learn why releasing the pain of the past is so difficult. You'll learn strategies to make letting go easier.

Everyone has been hurt in relationships. Few people can let that pain go so they can move on with their lives without the past mudding their joy. People tend to get caught in their anger and pain after they've been hurt. There are mental, emotional, and physical reasons why itis difficult to release this pain.

One area that can make it difficult to release the past is the misunderstanding of what forgiveness is. People often think forgiveness absolves the other person of anything that happened. You'll discover this is incorrect. Strategies and exercises to release the past range from recognizing your personal power, nurturing yourself, changing your thoughts, and discovering how to manage your feelings. In this book, you'll learn; Why forgiveness is crucial to your mental, emotional, and physical health • How childhood beliefs can interfere with releasing the past • You have the power within you to release the past • Forgiveness brings freedom • Strategies to assist you in forgiving and letting go.

Let me answer a few of your questions.

Are there requirements or prerequisites for this Book? There are no prerequisites for this Book. It's open to anyone who desires to know more about how to release the pain of the past.

Your success in this book depends on your ability to put the information into action. The information is simple, but understanding the information is insufficient. You must be willing to do the exercises and implement the strategies in your life.

What benefits will I receive from this book?

You'll learn why releasing the past is difficult and what you can do to make it easier for yourself. • You'll learn the emotional, mental, and physical causes of your pain. • You'll discover misconceptions about forgiveness. • You'll receive specific strategies and exercises to assist you in letting go of your pain and moving forward toward the life you want.

Is there a particular audience this book is geared toward?

This book is geared toward those who are tired of hurting from broken relationships, betrayals, and loss and are ready to take action to release that pain.

You will learn a valuable lesson. So, let's look at this book as a course that will assist us to navigate through life and the recovery of this trauma.

DONNIE & LATOYA NEAL

I've Decided to Live

MODULE 1

Why It's So Hard to Let Go of the Pain

There isn't a person in the world who hasn't been hurt by someone. Releasing the pain from these wounds is difficult for many, if not most. In this module, you'll learn how releasing the pain from the past is more complicated than just "getting over it." There are emotional, physical, and mental reasons why letting go of the past is so difficult.

Lesson 1

Understanding What Happens Emotionally

When you've been hurt by someone, there is more to the pain than "just" the one event. Emotions are a mish-mash of what has happened in the past, your pain in the present, your fears of the future, and your interpretation of what the event means about you.

Activating the Past

When you've experienced betrayal by one you love, it hurts deeply. It hurts so much you wonder if you can make it past what happened. Sometimes that pain is about more than that one event.

If someone betrayed you, the pain for all the times you were betrayed is awakened:

- ☒ You may not remember the events of the emotions triggered but they are still adding to the hurt you experience now.

- ☒ When you were betrayed in past relationships, no matter how old you were, that pain is stored in your body.

- ☒ **Your emotions don't care about the actual event. But they recognize the pain.** The pain of the past is awakened and rises, adding to the hurt. It's like the pain joins together in one big scream.

It's difficult to release the past when it's like a tangled chain and the pain of every betrayal you ever felt is attached to it.

The Loss of Dreams

Every relationship, job, or activity you enter into has dreams attached to it. Some of these dreams are small, such as going to a party and having an enjoyable time. Relationship dreams are huge. Often, they involve plans for the rest of your life.

When a relationship ends, everything you thought would happen in the future ends:

- Your dreams of loving this one special person and being loved by them is gone.

- Your dream, your expectation, that you would care and support each other through the difficult times has dissolved.

- Your dreams of security, caring, excitement, and your idea of family have disappeared.

Your hurt is increased by the repercussions in other parts of your life.

Your financial situation may change, and your career be negatively impacted. Additionally, you may lose friends and people you considered family if you've lost your partner.

Each additional consequence of the initial event complicates the feelings involved. These additional hurts make it more difficult to release the past and move on. No wonder letting go can be so difficult.

Loss of Your Sense of Self

It took time through the ups and downs of life to discover who you are. You may have felt comfortable with yourself and where life was doing and then "the big hurt" happened. Suddenly everything you thought you knew about yourself was shattered.

The ending of relationships is difficult. Ugly words are said, and accusations thrown about.

If you were in an emotionally abusive relationship, you must sort through what your partner said about you and what you believe to be true.

If you entered the relationship with a healthy self-esteem, you may feel embarrassed and even ashamed of where you are now. You'll need to spend time getting to know who you are without your partner telling you lies about yourself.

Sorting through the negativity and finding the truth about you will be a challenge, but one which will have you discovering the wonderful and delightful you.

You may feel on unstable ground as you get to know yourself again. It takes strength and courage to uncover the self you think you lost. That strength and courage is within you waiting to be rediscovered.

When you discover that your relationship was based upon a lie, you need to redefine yourself and your relationship. You'll feel the push to discover what is true and not true about your relationship. Part of moving on may be accepting you'll never know.

Before the big hurt, you may have defined yourself by your relationship. Suddenly that definition is no longer there.

Take time to discover the amazing person you are. Who you truly are is not based upon someone else's definition of you. Discover your own gifts and talents which are waiting for you to notice and use them.

You May Begin to Doubt Yourself

When you believe you've found the perfect person as partner or friend, and then that person leaves or betrays you, you begin to doubt yourself.

You may doubt your judgment. You may have thought you had good judgment about people but now you wonder if that's true.

It's not unusual to believe the fault lies with you.

Yes, soul searching may be needed, but know that rarely are

relationships all one person's fault unless one person has a mental or emotional disorder.

Your feelings about the relationship and about you are often deep and complex. This combination can make it difficult to release the past.

We'll discuss strategies to resolve these feelings in detail in a later lesson, so hang in there.

Summary

You've discovered that the following make it difficult to release the past:

1. Feelings from similar events increase the intensity of your feelings.

2. The loss of the future you dreamed about complicates your feelings of loss.

3. You may no longer know who you are, making it difficult to sort through your feelings.

4. You begin to doubt yourself.

Physical Effects of Being Hurt

In the next lesson you'll learn how your brain, brain chemicals, and hormones complicate being able to release the past.

Reflection Questions

To anchor in this lesson, please take the time to reflect on it and answer these reflection questions.

1. List at least 5 feelings you have about the pain you are feeling. List more if you can.

2. Write about how you've changed from before the painful event occurred to now.

3. How have your dreams for the future changed?

4. Do you have any doubts about yourself? If so, please list them.

Lesson 2

Understanding What Happens Physically

Not only do your emotions from similar past wounds combine with your most recent hurt, your body has chemical reactions which make releasing the past difficult. Your emotions trigger parts of your brain and the body's stress response increasing the difficulty.

This lesson is to show you that your emotional pain has a physical cause and difficulty releasing it isn't a weakness of character.

Your Brain Reacts Immediately

When you discover you've been betrayed, rejected, or your loved one is gone, your brain and body react immediately.

Your brain activates a series of physical responses resulting in chemical production that affects your thoughts and feelings:

1. **Your limbic or emotional brain reacts to your emotional pain or trauma.** This activated the stress response producing fear and anxiety.

2. **Extreme emotional trauma can result in PTSD (Post-traumatic stress disorder).** PTSD can make changes to the brain which can be long-lasting. The result is extreme emotional sensitivity affecting relationships with others, yourself, and your environment.

3. **Your prefrontal cortex, the thinking part of your brain, is stressed.** This makes it difficult to think clearly and may cause problems with your memory.

Emotional Pain Triggers Your Stress Response

Your body's response to loss and betrayal is ancient. You need people to survive both physically and emotionally.

Your body developed physical responses to help you stay alive. Many of these make it difficult to release painful feelings.

See how:

1. **Your stress response, also called Fight-Flight-Freeze, activates stress hormones:**

   ☒ **Adrenaline, produced by your adrenal glands on top your kidneys, is released.** Being rejected, betrayed, or losing your loved one is

   ☒ certainly stressful.

   ☒ **Adrenaline focuses your attention on the painful experience.** This focus makes letting go difficult.

   ☒ Norepinephrine, produced by the adrenal glands and the brain, is similar to adrenaline. Norepinephrine combined with adrenaline are designed to help you run away or fight to save your life.

   ☒ **The challenge with emotional wounds is that there's no place to run to.** You end up "stewing in your own juices," making it difficult to let go of what happened.

   ☒ Cortisol, activated by the brain and produced by the adrenal glands, is the stress hormone which does the most damage. It weakens your immune system, can mess up your digestion system, and can cause weight gain.

☒ These stress hormones can save your life when you need to react immediately, like jumping out of the path of a speeding car. With emotional pain, they interfere with your health and make it difficult to let go.

2. **Sex hormones are affected.** You might not think that emotional pain would affect your sex hormones, but it does.

☒ Estrogen increases in both men and women, making them more sensitive to stress. Since women have more estrogen to begin with, this affects women more.

☒ Higher estrogen levels in men lead to a decrease in testosterone.

☒ **High estrogen levels in both men and women lead to an increase in depression.** When depressed, it's more difficult to let go of the hurts and pains of the past.

3. **Neurotransmitters: Chemicals produced by the brain.**
   Your brain reacts immediately to every change in emotion.
   Your brain responds to your painful feelings by producing
   neurotransmitters which act with the other body chemicals
   discussed above.

   ☒ Dopamine, when you're stressed, acts on the very
   front part of your brain (prefrontal cortex) and
   makes it difficult to think straight. When you can't
   think straight, you can't logically think through
   what is happening to you.

   ☒ Acetylcholine can interfere with your sleep. When
   you can't sleep, you can't think well, you're more
   sensitive emotionally, and have greater difficulty
   handling the "ordinary" stresses of life.

   ☒ Glutamate is crucial for your brain and your health.
   **When you have too much, which can happen
   with the stress of betrayal and rejection,
   depression can be one of the side**
   effects.

   ☒ Gamma-aminobutyric acid (GABA) is wonderful for
   being calm and relaxed. When you have too much,
   as with extreme stress, the reaction is opposite,
   resulting in anxiety.

Summary

In this lesson, you've discovered some of the physical changes which occur during extreme emotional pain. These are changes you had no control over. Your body responded immediately to your emotional reaction to what happened.

The difficulty you've been having in releasing the past and moving forward is not your fault. You'll learn strategies to overcome what's happened in a later lesson.

Your Mental Reactions to Being Hurt

In the next lesson, you'll explore what happens mentally when you've been deeply wounded. This includes how your thinking processes have been affected.

Reflection

Before moving to the next lesson, spend a few minutes reflecting on how the emotional pain you've experienced affected you. Prepare for releasing the pain, by saying aloud the statements given. This prepares your subconscious mind.

For each question, think back to before you were hurt. Evaluate how much the following emotions have changed on a scale of 1 to 5.

1 - Not at all
2 - About 25% more
3 - About 50% more   .
4 - About 75% more
5 - 100% or more than before the hurt

1. Anxiety: _____

    Say aloud: Anxiety was chemically created by my body and I will be able to reduce it.

2. Depression: _____

    Say aloud: Depression was chemically created by my body and I will be able to reduce it.

3. Hopelessness: _____

    Say aloud: Hopelessness was chemically created by my body and I will be able to reduce it.

4. Mental Confusion: _____

    Say aloud: Mental Confusion was chemically created by my body and I will be able to reduce it.

Lesson 3

Understanding What Happens Mentally

Now that you know what happens emotionally and physically when you've experienced the deep pain of loss, it's time to look at what happens with your thoughts and how you process information.

The Power of Your Thoughts

When you've experienced a deep emotional wound, the natural response is to attempt to make sense of it.

Your thoughts cycle through many questions, such as:

1. Why?
2. What did I do?
3. How could this happen to me?
4. Am I being punished for something?

These questions spring from the raw pain you feel.

It's crucial to realize that your thoughts are so powerful that they can intensify your emotional pain by increasing the production of the chemicals we discussed in the last lesson.

You've already been hurt by someone else. Don't make the pain worse by your own thoughts. Recognize the areas which can sabotage your healing and discover how to stop them.

Three Common Ways You Harm Yourself with Your Thoughts

You can bring healing to yourself through your thoughts, or you can make life more miserable. Do any of these apply to you?

1. **You keep thinking about what happened.** When you're caught up in the emotions and memories of an event, your subconscious mind responds as it did when the event first occurred. It produces the same stress hormones, creates the same neurotransmitters, and makes the same tracings in your brain.

   ☒ **When you recall a painful event, you re-injure your brain.** Your brain and body respond just as it did when it first happened. Instead of being betrayed once, you are betrayed as often as you relive what happened.

⊠ **Find something wonderful and marvelous to think of** instead of reviewing the painful past.

2. **You make up stories to explain what happened.** Stick to the facts of the event. Don't make up anything as to why they did what they did. That just makes it worse.

3. Unless you were told, you just don't know.

   ⊠ When you make up stories about what happened, you're also creating feelings, which has your body making all those chemicals, which then has you feeling worse, which has your body making more chemicals, which...

   ⊠ **If you didn't see it or weren't told by the other person, precede your interpretation with "the story I'm making up is..."** This helps you realize that you just don't know.

4. **Your friends and family keep you stirred up.** You gotta love them. Your friends and family want to support you. They may be angry about what happened and let you know. They need to heal, and you need to heal.

   ⊠ At first this is supportive. If it continues, your feelings are stirred up and you relive the event again.

⊠ **Use these strategies to help you and your loved ones who want to support you:**

⊠ Let them know how much their support helped you.

⊠ Tell them, in order for you to heal, you need to quit reliving it. They may ask how you're doing, but please don't rehash the story.

⊠ Ask them to assist you by helping you to quit reliving the story. Give them something to say such as, "I'm glad to listen, but you did say you didn't want to relive what happened. How can I help you most right now?"

These strategies will assist you in breaking the habit of continuing to relive the painful event. Once you quit thinking about it, you can move back into happiness. (You'll learn more in Module 3.)

Summary

Your self-talk can support your healing or make it more difficult. Avoiding re-living the painful situation and asking others to not have you relive it will assist you in moving forward.

By managing your thoughts, you'll decrease the chemicals in your body which affect your attitude and mood.

Exploring Letting Go

In the next module, you'll explore the concept of forgiveness, what it is and what is isn't. Before moving on, please anchor in

this lesson by spending a few minutes with the following reflection questions.

Reflection

The following questions are designed to assist you in coming to know yourself better. Answer them as fully as you can.

1. Think back to someone who hurt you emotionally. How often did you keep re-living the situation? What did re-living the situation do to you?

2. What kinds of stories did you make up about what happened? Explore the motives you attached to the other person and what you made up as their thoughts about you.

3. Consider a time the support of family and friends kept the pain alive. Explore how their bringing up the event either helped or hurt you.

Lesson 4

Module 1 Summary and Reflection

The key to healing from emotional wounds is to be able to release the pain from those wounds.

In this module you learned there are three factors which make releasing the past difficult:

1. When you're hurt, your body responds by producing hormones and neurotransmitters which affect your emotions. You can become anxious and depressed.

2. The tendency is to keep thinking about what happened to you. This causes your brain to produce more hormones and neurotransmitters, resulting in greater anxiety and depression.

3. The emotions which resulted from what happened also continue the cycle.

To stop this cycle, you'll need to access your inner power, release the past, and form your new future.

In the next module, you'll learn that misconceptions about

forgiveness, the releasing of the past, may prevent you from letting go of what happened and moving forward.

Reflection

Before moving to the next module, spend time reflecting on what you've learned and discovering how it applies to you. This will prepare you for moving past your pain and moving into the wonderful future awaiting you.

1. What are the recurring thoughts of the past you don't want any more?

    Read each one of these recurring thoughts aloud and then say, "You're on notice. I don't want you anymore. You are going to leave now!"

2. What recurring feelings of the past do you not want anymore?

3. Out loud, tell each one of these feelings: "You are not going to be part of my life anymore."

Choose the correct answer.

1.   You'll get the most from this course if you:

    A.   Pick and choose lessons at your leisure

    B.   Study the quiz prior to working through the lessons

    C.   Read the lessons, skip the activities, and take the quiz

    D.   Do the lessons in sequential order

2.   Present hurts bring up pain from past similar hurts.

    A.   True

    B.   False

3.   A deep emotional hurt can:

    A.   Have you doubt yourself

    B.   Make your future uncertain

    C.   Cause you to lose your sense of self

    D.   All of the above

4.   Your brain waits 5 minutes before reacting to emotional pain.

    A.   True

    B.   False

5.   When you've been emotionally hurt, your body produces:

    A.   Oxytocin

    B.   Iron

    C.   Neurotransmitters

    D.   Heat

6.   When emotional pain triggers your stress response, the following happens:

A. You go into Fight-Flight-Freeze mode

B. You go dancing

C. You crave coffee

D. You get a tattoo

7. Some neurotransmitters have the opposite effect when there's too much of it.

A. True

B. False

8. Regarding your thoughts about your deep hurt:

A. They can make your brain act as if you've been hurt again.

B. Failure is an opportunity to beat yourself up emotionally.

C. It's a good excuse to look for some pity.

D. All the above

9. Making up stories about what happened can:

   A. Get you a movie deal

   B. Make you hurt worse

   C. Help you heal

   D. Convince others to get on your side

10. When family and friends keep talking about what happened:

   A. Ask them to support you by not talking about it.

   B. Tell them you appreciate their support.

   C. Ask them to remind you not to talk about it, if you do
       start talking about it.

   D. All of the above

Answer Key

1.   D

2.   A

3.   D

4.   B

5.   C

6.   A

7.   A

8.   A

9.   B

10.   D

Module 2

Understanding Forgiveness

The number and type of hurts you've suffered in the past, combined with your thoughts and beliefs, can make it difficult to release the past. When you add the biochemical response of your body, it's a wonder anyone can forgive another.

In this module, you'll learn that your view of forgiveness can add to the difficulty of putting the past behind you. In this short module, you'll explore what forgiveness is and what forgiveness isn't. This knowledge will assist you in letting go of the hurt and moving forward with your life in joy.

Lesson 5

What Forgiveness Is Not

The emotions, thoughts, beliefs, and chemical nature of your body make it difficult to release the past, to forgive. The memory of what happened will be with you. **The key to healing is releasing the anger and resentment surrounding the event.**

Even for the deepest of wounds, it's crucial to find a way to detach as much as possible from the pain. In most cases this means to move into a state of forgiveness of the one who caused the wound.

Many people are resistant to forgiveness because they don't understand what forgiveness is. Before you explore what forgiveness is, let's look at what it isn't.

What Forgiveness Is Not

If you're told that you must forgive someone to release the past and gain peace, you're likely to angrily reply, "It wasn't my fault. Why do I have to be the one to forgive?"

Within that reaction is the thought that forgiveness is about saying that the person who did the hurting has no responsibility for their actions and the consequences of their actions.

Consider these important principles relating to forgiveness:

1. **Forgiveness is not about the other person.** When you forgive someone, including yourself, you're not saying that person has no responsibility for what happened. Their actions caused pain and, yes, they are responsible for that pain.

   ☒ Even if they completely accept the responsibility for their actions, that doesn't take away your pain. Even if they tell you how sorry they are 100 times, that won't take away your pain.

   ☒ **You are the one who holds that pain, and you are the one who will need to let it go.** No, it's not fair, but it is true.

   ☒ Forgiveness is completely about you. It's about your freedom, your peace, and your future.

2. **Forgiveness is not about staying with someone who is toxic.** A major misconception about forgiveness is that you then must be with the person who harmed you, even if that person is toxic.

   ☒ You don't need to be with someone who emotionally, physically, or sexually abuses you, lies continually, is drunk or high much of the time, or steals from you, whether they steal things, your self-respect, or your dignity.

⊠ **You don't have to be friends with or spend time with people who cause you to feel terrible about yourself.** Forgiveness doesn't require this.

⊠ Your job is to care for yourself and those you're responsible for. You can forgive the person, release the anger and emotional pain, and never see them again.

3. **Forgiveness does not mean you have to trust someone who has betrayed you again... and again... and again.**

⊠ Recognize that many people have an addiction. This addiction could be to substances, shopping, sex, gambling, even lying. An active addict has characteristics which are part of the disease, and you only see those characteristics when they're using.

⊠ They lie even when the truth would do better. They're irresponsible. They'll take care of their addiction first and not pay attention to you. They steal. And they won't even notice when they've hurt you.

⊠ There are also those who have personality disorders. They can ruin your self-esteem, cause you to doubt yourself, and convince you that what you know you saw or heard is not true.

- ☒ You may release your pain by forgiving them but remember who they are. They can't help themselves. Accept that and stay away from them if possible.

4. **Forgiveness isn't giving away your power or making you weak.** Making the choice to forgive someone is one of the most powerful things you can do for yourself.

Anyone can hold onto anger. Comparatively few can truly forgive. That is the topic of the next lesson.

Summary

In this lesson, you've learned the basics of what forgiveness is not. **It's the misunderstanding of what forgiveness is that blocks most people from attaining freedom from the deep hurts they've suffered in life.**

Before moving to the next lesson and learning what forgiveness is, take a few moments to anchor in what you've learned.

Reflection

Please answer these questions as fully as you can:

1. What is your biggest concern about forgiving the person who hurt you the most?

2. Everyone has done something they are ashamed of. What is your biggest fear if you forgive yourself?

3. List all the reasons you have for not forgiving that one person who has hurt you so badly.

Lesson 6

What Forgiveness Is

Now that you know that forgiveness isn't about spending time with toxic people or giving away your power, it's time to look at what forgiveness is.

Very simply, forgiveness is FREEDOM.

- ☒ Freedom from having what happened always on your mind
- ☒ Freedom the anger and fear
- ☒ Freedom from having to grit your teeth when you see them

As difficult as forgiveness can be, it lightens the load on your mind, brings peace to your heart, and frees you to move forward to the future.

Refusing Forgiveness Affects All Areas of Your Life

Holding onto pain and resentment has major negative effects upon you. You'll find you're easily distracted by the pain, and this limits your ability to be fully productive. You also miss the

joys of life.

When you relive what happened, your body reacts as if you just experienced the pain. You feel like a victim and have difficulty accessing your inner strength.

Holding onto emotional pain weakens you. You are like the powerful elephant prevented from moving because it believes the little chain around its ankle controls its life.

Let's examine more deeply what forgiveness gives you:

1. **Forgiveness gives you the power to move into the future.** When you're hurt, no matter how badly, you can feel like you're carrying around a ball and chain. You hold it so tightly that you've forgotten how to release it. If you allow it, that wound can lock you into pain and keep you from seeing the beauty in life.

   ☒ **When you release the pain, you unchain yourself and throw away the chain and everything attached to it.**

   ☒ Your body responds with an "Ahhh" and releases energy. This allows you to make plans for the future and open your heart to reviving neglected relationships and meeting new people.

2. **No longer are you defined by your wound.** Forgiveness allows you to be the amazing, wonderful person you are. Before you release the pain from that terrible hurt, you're defined as the one whose partner betrayed you, or whose boss falsely accused and fired you.

   ☒ Avoid being defined by what happened to you. Define yourself by overcoming what happened and being more successful and happier than anyone thought you could be.

   ☒ **When you're not focusing on the past, you'll find your path to happiness, the gift and talents you've forgotten, and the strength to look fear in the eye and go right through it.**

   ☒ The pain will have changed you, but when you release it, *you* choose to determine what happens to you, not someone else.

3. **When you forgive, the other person no longer has control of you.**

   ☒ When you don't forgive, the person who hurt you has control of you. They're on your mind, occupying your thoughts, sapping your energy, perhaps determining where you go, who you see and what you do... and they don't have to say a word.

⊠ Enough of that. Choose to not let them control your thoughts and emotions. Letting it all go demonstrates that they can't control you. You control what you hold onto and what you release.

4. **You get to make the powerful choice of releasing the pain and moving into freedom.**

⊠ You'll no longer be caught in victim consciousness. Victim consciousness has you believing you are powerless, making it difficult for you to take positive steps for the future.

⊠ You demonstrate what a powerful person you are to let something go that many people can't. **It takes great personal power to forgive.**

⊠ No longer will you be hyper vigilant, fearing similar injuries in relationships. **Your true self will shine through improving current and future relationships.**

5. **Your physical health improves.** When you forgive, there are powerful changes in the body which lead to a healthier and longer life.

⊠ In the last few decades, biologists and medical researchers have discovered the power of the mind-body connection. They have found that holding onto emotional pain affects the body mentally, emotionally and physically.

☒ **The Mayo Clinic, one of the premier medical clinics in the world, identifies the following changes with forgiveness:**

☒ Lower blood pressure

☒ Stronger immune system

☒ Better heart health

☒ Less stress, which improves digestion, sexual response, sleep, and more

☒ Lower risk of anxiety and depression

☒ Improved relationships, which is known to strengthen your immune system, increase the "feel good" chemicals in your body, and reduce stress

As you can see, forgiving someone is one of the most powerful choices you can make to improve your life physically, mentally, emotionally, and spiritually. This makes positive changes in your relationships.

Summary

Now that you know the positive effects forgiveness can have in every area of your life, the question you may be asking is, "How

do I forgive?" In the next module, you'll explore various methods which have proven to assist in forgiveness. **The key is finding the one which works for you.**

Before moving to the next lesson, please spend a few minutes right now to reflect on and anchor in what you've learned in this lesson.

Reflection

1. Think of someone who has hurt you and you haven't forgiven. Notice what happens to your body and how your thoughts and emotions change. Now write about what you noticed.

2. Recall someone you love and feel comfortable with. Notice the changes in your body, mind, and emotions. List what you've noticed.

3. What do you want to achieve by forgiving someone?

Lesson 7

Module 2 Summary and Reflection

Now, you know it's not true that letting go of the past, also known as forgiveness, doesn't make you a victim and doesn't mean that someone unhealthy for you must stay in your life.

Forgiveness benefits all areas of your life. Your emotional and physical health will improve. You'll be able to think more clearly and move into the future with confidence and joy.

Now, all you need to know is how to accomplish this healing and life-giving process. That's what you'll learn in the next module.

To prepare for what comes next, please take a few minutes right now to reflect on the following. This will prepare your subconscious mind for your next step into personal power.

Reflection

Allow yourself to answer the following as fully as you can. Write what comes to you. Allow your mind to flow.

1. When I am no longer saddled with the pain of "it," I'll be able to:

2. Write out why a future without emotional pain is better than feeling the way you do now.

Module 2 Quiz

Choose the correct answer.

1.   When you forgive someone, you show how weak you are.

     A.   True

     B.   False

2.   By not forgiving you:

     A.   Weaken your immune system

     B.   Live in the past

     C.   Sap your energy

     D.   All the above

3.   Forgiveness means you must stay with someone who is dangerous.

     A.   True

B.   False

4.   Forgiveness:

A.   Shows you're weak

B.   Puts the one who hurt you in control

C.   Is about your freedom from pain

D.   Means you should trust someone who lies

5.   Forgiveness strengthens your health.

A.   True

B.   False

6.   Forgiveness:

A.   Is stupid

B.   Prevents you from doing what you want

C.   Allows you to choose what you want

to do without worrying about the other person

D.   Increases anxiety and depression

7.   Forgiveness takes more strength than holding onto the pain.

A.   True

B.   False

8.   Forgiveness can:

A.   Improve your relationships

B.   Make you feel more powerful

C.   Allow you to have more freedom

D.   All the above

9.   When you forgive someone, do you have to tell them
     10. Forgiveness is for?
     that you forgave them?
     A. You
     B. The Person Who Hurt You
     C. Making your family feel better
     D. Making your friends feel better

Answer Key

1. B
2. D
3. B
4. C
5. A
6. C
7. A
8. D
9. B
10. A

Write Your Thoughts

Module 3

Strategies to Let The Pain Go

You now know why it's difficult to release or forgive the past. You also know why forgiveness is so very important for you. The question you are left with is, "If forgiving is difficult and good for me, how do I let all the pain go?"

In this module, you'll be introduced to several activities and techniques to assist you in forgiving and releasing the past. Some will appeal to you and others won't. Choose the two or three which you can relate to and use them to achieve peace.

Know this about you: You can do this!!!

Lesson 8

Recognize How Powerful You Are

The evidence that forgiveness is one of the biggest gifts you can give yourself is overwhelming. Forgiveness strengthens your health and brings peace to you in mind and spirit. You've also learned why forgiveness is difficult.

You can do this! You have everything you need within you to discover how you can release the pain and forgive. You are more powerful than you ever thought you were. All you need to do is access that power and bring it forward.

You Have the Opportunity to Access Your Inner Power

The power you have has nothing to do with how powerful you feel. Even those you believe have accomplished much in their lives may not feel powerful.

You feel powerful when you have control over your inner world:

1. When you control your thoughts, you control your emotions and how you respond in life.

2. When you control your emotions, you control your thoughts and your response to the difficulties of life.

3. When you control the way you respond, you control your thoughts and feelings about the situation.

4. **When you control your thoughts, feelings and response, you're able to keep the situation from becoming worse.**

When you don't have inner control, you're more likely to have a tendency to say and do things you later regret. Learn from those experiences.

As you work with the exercises in the lessons that follow, you'll learn how to control your thoughts, feelings, and responses. You'll be accessing and using the amazing power you have within you.

These concepts are key. Keep reading them until you can repeat them without hesitation:

1. **Whatever happened to you does not diminish who you are.** Unless you suffered a severe physical injury, you still have the talents and abilities you had before the

   pain entered your life. If your life has been filled with challenges, you may not have yet discovered how amazing you are.

- ☒ When you release the pain, you'll feel more "you" than you've ever felt. When your inner vision isn't distorted with the past, you can discover your gifts, talents, and inner resources.

2. **You are the most important person in whatever happened.** Your well-being, inner peace, and health are all that's important in this process. Focus on yourself and what you need to do to achieve that peace.

   - ☒ If you're concerned about whoever else was involved, put them aside as you work through the following exercises.

   - ☒ **When you release the past, you will have the strength and energy to handle whatever is awaiting you.**

3. **What you do and say is about you.** What the others involved do and say is about them.

   - ☒ Remember who is most important right now: *you.* Don't allow what others say to you or about you distract you from what's important.

   - ☒ If you have family or friends who believe they're doing you a favor by keeping you updated on

     the others involved, ask them to stop. What they're saying is not important, at least for now.

4. **Releasing the past may not be easy, but you can do it.**
    Whether you're building a skyscraper or releasing the pain
    of the past, all are accomplished the same way: step by
    step.

    ☒ Although you know your ultimate goal, focus on
    each step and the rest will fall into place. **Make a
    commitment to yourself now to do the
    exercises.**

5. **You'll be redefining yourself.** When the pain of what
    happened has been with you a long time, you may
    subconsciously define yourself by your pain. Be willing to
    release not only the pain, but also the way the pain defined
    you.

    ☒ **No matter what happened, you can be happy
    again.** No matter what happened, you can be
    successful again. No matter what happened, you
    can have a loving and fulfilling relationship. Yes,
    life will be different, but it isn't over.

Summary

You have within you the power and ability to achieve your desire
to release the past. Make a commitment to yourself to do the
exercises. The rest will fall into place.

Before moving to the next lesson, where you'll begin focusing your mind on letting go, take a few minutes to review and reflect on what you've learned about your power to release the past by forgiving.

Reflection

The following questions are designed to assist you incorporate what you've learned in this lesson.

1. Describe how you want to experience your inner power.

2. Why is it crucial for you to focus on yourself as you do the exercises?

How has what happened defined who you are? How do you want that to change?

Lesson 9
Align Your Beliefs to Releasing Pain

You learned in the last lesson that you have the personal power to release your emotional pain through forgiveness. All you need to do is follow the exercises. Take them one step at a time.

In this lesson you'll begin your journey by aligning your beliefs to your goal of releasing all that pain. You'll do this by giving direct messages to your subconscious mind. This lays the foundation for the other exercises which follow.

Give Your Subconscious Mind Directions
You may not know it, but your subconscious mind runs your life. You know those things you do automatically? That's your subconscious mind at work making your life easier.

Your subconscious mind can also make life difficult when it's working with outdated information. That information was great when you were a child. It may have been exactly what you wanted last week, but this week you need something different.

You can upgrade the data in your subconscious mind easily by telling it the following:

1. How you want your life to look
2. What you want to hear from others and yourself
3. The types of feelings you want to have
4. What smells you want
5. What you want to taste

Just like a software upgrade for a particular program, this upgrade is for a specific belief. You're going to be installing within your subconscious mind the beliefs (the software) you need to achieve your goal of eliminating the painful past from your life.

Upgrading The Beliefs In Your Subconscious Mind

There are two steps to upgrading your beliefs. The first is identifying the beliefs you want to change. The second step is deciding what beliefs you want to place within your subconscious mind.

In Module 1 you explored why it's difficult to release the pain from the past. This difficulty may be due to thoughts and feelings based upon beliefs about forgiveness. It's important to identify these old beliefs.

Examples of old beliefs to upgrade are:

- Why do I have to forgive? They're the ones who hurt me.

- If I forgive them, they'll have power to hurt me again.

- I don't deserve to forgive myself.

Determine Your New Belief

Identify the new belief you want as your upgrade. Your new belief is a variation of the opposite of the old belief.

Using the old beliefs above you'll want to upgrade to:

- I forgive so that I'll have inner peace.

- Forgiveness allows me to have control over my life.

- When I forgive, the one who hurt me stays out of my thoughts.

- I deserve to have the peace which comes from releasing the past.

You might notice these new beliefs resemble affirmations. Use the process below to install your affirmations into your subconscious mind.

Install Your New Beliefs

Your subconscious mind only understands concrete information. If you use abstract words such as "forgive" and "love," your subconscious mind needs cues from your five senses to tell it what you mean.

Let's go through the process step-by-step:

1. **Write down the belief you want.** For this example, we'll use "I forgive so I'll have inner peace." Both "forgive" and "inner peace" are abstract concepts.

- **Write out two things you'll see in your life when forgiveness brings inner peace.** This needs to be something you'll see as if you were watching a video or looking at a photo.

- Perhaps inner peace means you can now go to a restaurant you've avoided because you didn't want to see your ex. You'd write out in sensory detail what going to the restaurant looks like.

- "We're at My Favorite Pizza. (sight) The smell of pizza cooking in the over is yeasty. (smell) My mouth waters. (tactile) My friends and I are laughing. (sound) The pizza is hot and spicy just as I like it. (taste & touch) Everyone there is smiling and eating."

2. **What will you overhear people saying about you when this belief is active in your life?** The comments are about what people notice about you now that you're at peace.

   - "I haven't seen her looking this relaxed in ages!"

   - "Look at that smile on his face!"

3. **What will you say about yourself?**

   - "It's great to be able to have fun again!"

4. **What are you feeling?** This will be an emotion which is abstract. You'll give concrete examples giving your subconscious mind a way to identify the emotion.

(Examples follow.) First identify the feeling. We'll use the example of "happy:"

Think of a time you last felt that emotion. *When I hit the home run*

- Where did you feel it in your body? *In my head*

- What color is the feeling? *Yellow*

- What's its shape? *A fountain*

- What's its texture? *Rough*

- What does it smell like? *Like newly mowed grass*

- What does it taste like? *Peppermint*

- What's its temperature? *Warm*

The Secret That Few People Know

Once you've filled in all the information, say the belief to yourself and, while speaking it, tap on your forehead three times, then your heart three times.

This "awakens" your brain and your heart to recognize the belief and store it in your subconscious mind.

Summary

Now that you know how to install new beliefs in your subconscious mind, fill out the worksheet from your Additional Resources box for the beliefs listed. Make copies of the worksheets so you can use them whenever you need.

After the beliefs are installed, move to the next exercise to learn how to change the way you think.

Reflection

Use the worksheet below for this lesson to install the following beliefs.

1. I achieve peace when I forgive.

2. Forgiveness puts me in control of my life.

3. Forgiveness releases my emotional pain.

4. I deserve to forgive myself.

5. When I forgive, I have the energy to live a new life.

Lesson 10

Think Your Way to Freedom

Now that you've installed beliefs in your subconscious mind on forgiving and releasing the past pain, it's time to use those beliefs.

The next two lessons address the two major contributors to your pain: thoughts and emotions. In this lesson you'll learn strategies to control your thoughts as well as a powerful "trick" to command you into thinking what you want.

Your Conscious Mind Can Be an Unruly Child

Your conscious mind is easily distracted. You have the power to get your mind to "sit down and be still." Although your subconscious mind is set with the new beliefs, it's time to train it.

It's time for the real YOU to get in control of the unruly part of you which enjoys running amok and causing chaos.

Try these tricks and techniques to get your conscious mind, your thoughts, under control:

1. **The trick of being two different people.** This is like having two parts of yourself battling for control. **You want your healthy self to win.** Here's one way.

⊠ Stand tall in front of the mirror. This is your strong and powerful self who knows that you can release the pain of the past. Look yourself in the eye. You're looking at the you who's in pain.

⊠ In a strong commanding voice say, "**It's over. It happened in the past. It's not going to change. It's time to move on.**" Of course, adapt these words to suit you.

⊠ You might hear or feel this whiney little voice start to say, "But, I...," interrupt the voice and say in a strong voice, "**No, I don't want to hear it. We have a life to live. Now let it go.**"

⊠ When you command out loud, you're reinforcing the beliefs you installed in your subconscious mind. You're telling your subconscious mind, "Yes, I really mean that I am ready to release the past and move to a healthy future."

2. **Put all your thoughts and pain in a letter.... Then burn it.** Research shows that writing things out with pen and paper has a positive effect upon the brain.

⊠ **Pull out pen and paper and write a letter you won't be sending.** No one will see this except you, so have no worries about how it looks or how you spell.

⊠ Write a letter to whomever hurt you. You can write to a person, an organization, God, even to you.

⊠ **Put all your feelings into that letter.** Use whatever language you want. Make it as strong as you can. Put the letter somewhere safe for a day.

⊠ A day later, pull the same letter out. As you read it, cross out words and make them even stronger. Let all your anger, frustration, and pain come out in that letter. Put it aside for a day.

⊠ Same thing as the past two days. Put it aside for a day.

⊠ Take the letter out. Read it one more time. When finished, say aloud, "**I release and let you go. You have no more power over me. Be gone.**" Then burn it.

⊠ This process engages both your conscious and subconscious mind. Give it a try, putting aside your doubts about whether or not it will work.

3. **Change your thoughts. Reliving painful events only reinjures you.** Have your strong powerful self who wants to be free of the past talk sternly, but lovingly, to the part of you who is hurting.

☒ Say, "Stop it. We're not going there." Then say, "Remember, this is where we're going." Begin imagining in all the sensory detail one of those wonderful images you used earlier when installing your beliefs.

☒ Avoid the temptation to be frustrated when you "catch" yourself rehashing the past. You'll catch yourself earlier each time until you rarely need to speak sternly to yourself.

Avoid Allowing Others to Bring You Down

Friends and family may say or do things they believe are supportive but don't realize they're triggering the memories and feelings you're ready to release. When that happens, it's time to take firm but loving action.

If it's appropriate, tell the person who's making the comments, "Thank you for your continued support. If you would, I'd appreciate you supporting me by not bringing it up again. Let's just talk about how wonderful life is now."

If their comments trigger the feelings, give yourself a pep talk. "Shake it off. You're doing great. Let's go over again what life will be like when this is gone." Then review one of your images you used when installing beliefs... or develop a new one.

Always remember how amazing you are and that you can release the pain and move to a happier future.

Summary

Congratulations on learning strategies in how to talk to yourself and change the way you think.

In the next lesson, you'll learn how to change the feelings which bring you down.

Before you go on to the next lesson, please take a few minutes now to reflect and anchor in what you've learned.

Reflection

It's time for action. Please do the following now.

1. Write out the words you're going to tell your hurting self that it's time to move on to a better life

2. Now, go to your mirror and say what you wrote. Write down what you experienced.

Lesson 11

Tame the Pain

Now that you've learned ways to manage your thoughts, it's time to gain control of your emotions. You took the first step in the last lesson. Thoughts produce emotions.

Most people are surprised when they learn they can change emotions. Sometimes it seems emotions "just appear." They are actually triggered. You have the power and ability to tame those painful emotions. The skills you learned in the last lesson have prepared you for this lesson.

Feelings Are Important

Before you learn how to change feelings, it's crucial to know that feelings aren't bad. **Feelings are a natural human response to what happens in life.** They are a signal of what brings joy and where you are hurting.

For example, if you're with friends and someone brings up getting married, you could recall fondly your own marriage, or you could feel sadness because you're not married and would like to be.

What may be happy to one person may remind you of someone or something painful. Knowing how to work with your feelings when this happens is empowering. **These feelings aren't bad; they're painful.**

The Role of Grief

Whenever you experience a loss, you move through the stages of grief. The loss could range from scuffing your new shoes to the horror of betrayal. The stages of grief are the same for both but more intense for the more painful and life-changing event.

When you scuff your shoes, you'll go through the stages quickly and, probably, once. When you've been betrayed, you go back and forth through the various stages with changes in the type and intensity of feelings.

The more deeply you've been hurt, the longer it takes to navigate the stages of grief. Be patient with yourself as you use the tools below to navigate through the feelings.

Take Care of Your Long-Term Health

When in the midst of the pain of grief, it's difficult to think about the consequences of your feelings on your physical, mental, and emotional health.

It's crucial for your long-term emotional and physical health to feel, work through, and release the feelings which come

from grief. In cases of betrayal or the ending of a relationship, it takes time to navigate those feelings.

For your emotional, mental, and physical health, it's important to release the anger, anxiety, and despair which can accompany loss. The sooner you're able to do this, the more quickly you can move on to your new future.

Adapting What You've Learned to Release Destructive Feelings

Discover how to adapt what you learned in managing your thoughts to learning how to change your feelings:

1. **The Mirror.** In the early stages after someone has betrayed, abandoned, or otherwise hurt you, it's important to encourage and support yourself. **As you stand in front of the mirror looking yourself in the eye, say aloud to yourself:**

    ☒ "Yes, this is terrible, but you will make it through this."

- ☒ "Yes, (whatever you need to say about the situation), but you will make it through this."

- ☒ **After about a month or so, change your messages to:**

- ☒ "It's over. Let it go and move on."

- ☒ "They're not worth staying stuck. Let's get moving."

- ☒ When you do this, you are telling your subconscious mind, "Yes, I recognize this is difficult, but I know I'll get better."

2. **Put all your feelings in a letter.... Then burn it.**

- ☒ Use the same process you used in releasing thoughts. This time, focus on your feelings.

- ☒ When you're ready to burn the letter, say, "**I release this relationship, this situation, and all my associated feelings. I'm beginning a new life!**"

- ☒ Remember to write long-hand and not with a computer. This method is an excellent way to get those feelings out.

3. **Change your feelings.** It doesn't matter where your feelings come from, you can change them. Learning to

change your feelings requires some advanced preparation.

- ☒ Recall at least three wonderful memories.

- ☒ Write each one out in detail using all five senses. Get in touch with the feelings you had at that event.

- ☒ When you catch yourself feeling miserable, tell yourself, "Nope, I'm not going to waste this time on feelings that make me miserable."

- ☒ Immediately recall one of those three happy memories. Immerse yourself in that memory until the other feeling is gone.

- ☒ Because of the way the brain works, focusing on the happy and wonderful feeling cancels out the unhappy one. **The more you do this the more your brain is trained to focus on the positive.**

Summary

As you learned how to change your feelings, you noticed that the exercises were similar to the one of changing thoughts. **Thoughts produce feelings.**

In the next lesson, you'll learn how to change your behavior so you can release the past and move to the future.

Before you go to the next lesson, please take time now to do the following exercise to anchor in what you've learned.

Reflection

Take the time now to write out the wonderful memories you'll use to knock out the painful memories. Put in as much sensory detail as possible. Include:

- ☒ How it looked (colors, shapes)
- ☒ How it sounded (voices, music, people's comments)
- ☒ How it felt (your own feelings and how your body felt)
- ☒ How it smelled
- ☒ How it tasted (foods, drink, imagine tasting something there like a blade of grass)

1. Describe an event in which you were proud.

2. Describe an event in which you were excited.

3. Describe an event in which you were peaceful.

Lesson 12

Changing Behavior

By reading the lessons and doing the exercises, you have strategies to change the thoughts and feelings which resulted from holding onto the pain of the past.

The last area to be aware of is your own behavior. Repetitive actions become a habit. Habits are actions which occur without thought. Recovery from the past requires that you apply thought to your actions and behaviors.

Know the Definition of Insanity

If you want to buy a vegetarian meal but always go to the steak house which puts bacon into its vegetables, you're never going to get a vegetarian meal. Every time you go to that restaurant wanting vegetarian, you'll be disappointed. That's an example of insanity.

Insanity is repeatedly doing the same thing expecting different results.

If you continue to go to the same park you and your ex always went to, and you leave that park feeling down or angry each time, you're the living example of insanity. True, you may feel like you're going insane with all the pain you're carrying, but there's no reason to make it worse.

To recover from the painful wound you've experienced, it's time to embrace the challenge of finding new things to do, new places to go, and new ways of doing things.

From Insanity to Victimization

Many people are examples of the definition of insanity. They also begin to feel like a victim because nothing is working out for them. You may have felt like a victim when the relationship ended. **You don't need to remain a victim.**

What happens after everything pertaining to the relationship is over, is that you are left with a major challenge. That challenge is to pull yourself out of feeling like a victim and get back in touch with the amazing, powerful you that is hiding beneath all that pain.

You are the one who can pull yourself out of repetitive and non-productive behaviors and become the wonderful you.

Behaviors Can Trigger Thoughts and Emotions

Your actions can assist in your goal to release the past or they can hold the past firmly in place. It's crucial to be aware of what behaviors trigger the emotional pain. **Once you know your**

triggers, stay away from them. That's more difficult than you think, but you can do it.

Find New Things to Talk About

Avoid talking about the painful event with almost everyone. Talking about what happened brings up the feelings. Confine your discussion about "the event" and the person involved to your therapist, coach, spiritual leader, or support group.

Best friends, family, and those who enjoy hearing gossip won't help you. Your friends and family want to give advice and support, but it may keep the pain going.

Someone objective assists in moving past the pain. They'll point out where you're continuing to hurt yourself and how to stop.

If you still have the need to "talk," use the releasing exercise where you work on the same letter three times and then burn it. Repeat that process as often as needed.

Go New Places

If you always went to Joe's Pizza, it's time to get acquainted with Penelope's Pizza. If you always ordered pepperoni and pineapple pizza, it's time to order a different kind. Better yet, go to a cooking class and learn to make something new and different.

If you always went to a particular movie theater or at a particular time, go to another theater, unless you only went to the theater for them. Then don't go to the theater at all.

You may wonder why you need to change the places you go. You don't need to change anything as long as they don't resurrect the pain of the past. If being there continues to hurt you, **quit doing what hurts.**

Music Is a Powerful Memory Trigger

As much as you loved that song you shared, it's time to let it go. The memories associated with it can resurrect the experience of loss quickly. This is true for any music. Find new songs about your new life.

Quit Attempting to Figure Out What Went Wrong Unless You're with a Therapist

It's natural to want to know what you could have done differently. To discover what went wrong, you often need a therapist or relationship coach.

Just remember that you can't change the past, but you can apply your new knowledge to change your future.

Summary

Congratulations on almost finishing this course.

You've learned what happens in your brain when you're hurt emotionally. You've also learned why forgiveness, or letting go, is important.

You now have powerful tools and tips to change your thoughts and emotions so you can release the pain as quickly as possible. Then, you learned in this lesson the importance of changing certain behaviors, so those thoughts and emotions aren't triggered.

Before you celebrate the completion of this course, take a few minutes to answer the reflection questions so you can anchor in what you've learned.

Reflection

Please write out your answers to the following questions.

1. What activities result in painful memories?

2. What can you do instead?

3. What are the qualities of the wonderful you that you're ready to find again? List as many as you can.

Lesson 13

Module 3 Summary and Reflection

In this module you've learned the tools and strategies which will assist in changing thoughts, feelings, and behaviors which anchor in the past. You now know that managing those three things comes when you access your personal power.

As you use the strategies in this module, you'll find the pain lessening. Your mind will clear, and you can focus on what's important to you. You'll be able to move into your new future.

Reflection

Describe what you'd do in the following situations:

1. You're out to lunch and the person who hurt you runs right into you. Your gut clenches and feelings of worthlessness pop up. What can you do immediately and what can you do later?

2. You're at a party and someone speaks in glowing terms about the person who betrayed you. The old hurt comes roaring back. What can you do to release the pain?

3. After the party where someone was talking glowingly about the person who hurt you, you can't quit thinking about what happened. What can you do?

4. Your route to work takes you past a place that reminds you of "the big hurt." Each time you feel sad. What can you do?

Module 3 Quiz

Choose the correct answer.

1. You don't always know how powerful you are.

    A. True

    B. False

2. Who is most important in the process of forgiving?

    A. The others involved

    B. You

    C. Your friends

    D. Your family

3. When you release the past and forgive, you'll:

    A. Redefine yourself

    B. Tap into your inner power

C.   Keep the situation from getting worse

D.   All the above

4.   Sometimes you need to tell loved ones how to support you as you're healing from the pain of the past.

A.   True

B.   False

5.   Looking in the mirror and commanding myself to "get over it":

A.   Proves I have a split personality

B.   Reinforces the belief that I can and will release the past

C.   Is a sign I'm crazy

D.   Convinces me it's time for ice cream

6. Controlling my thoughts prevents me from reinforcing the pain of the past.

    A. True

    B. False

7. I can change my feelings by:

    A. Remembering times when I felt proud of myself

    B. Crying in our favorite pizza place

    C. Listening to our favorite song over and over again

    D. Hitting myself on the head with a rubber hose

8. I change my behavior by:

    A. Doing new things

    B. Finding new favorite places to go

    C. Discovering new music I enjoy

D.   All the above

9.   Whether I know it or not, I have the personal power to release the past and move into a wonderful future.

A.   True

B.   False

10.   The following will help me to forgive and release the past:

A.   My inner strength

B.   My determination to be happy

C.   Doing the exercises in the lessons

D.   All of the above

Answer Key

1. A

2. B

3. D

4. A

5. B

6. A

7. A

8. D

9. A

10. D

The Conclusion

You are now ready to live again. No matter what the circumstances are, there is life after this. Life sometimes gets difficult, but nevertheless, you are still who you are called to be. You do not have to live your life in defeat. Sometimes situations happen to expose us to who we really are. We cannot appreciate strength until we understand what it is to be weak. You can now value your joy because you endured your pain. You no longer have to accept that you are a victim, but rather a conqueror. Yes, it happen, yes it was real, yes it did hurt. I no longer live in that place, and I am ready to get up and live. So I leave you with this..........I've decided to LIVE!!!

NOTES

NOTES

NOTES

.

Made in the USA
Middletown, DE
19 September 2022

10749234R00055